Of Fire and Ice

DARON KENNETH

AuthorHouse™
1663 Liberty Drive
Bloomington, IN 47403
www.authorhouse.com
Phone: 1 (800) 839-8640

Published by AuthorHouse 11/07/2017

ISBN: 978-1-5462-1219-5 (sc)
ISBN: 978-1-5462-1218-8 (e)

Print information available on the last page.

This book is printed on acid-free paper.

Contents

A Day Without Sun

As I sit on the back porch, I can see
The sun isn't going to shine today.
For today is just a lonely day in February.
The snow has gone away for at least today.
The poor trees look so bare and cold
Just standing there alone. The roads
Are all covered with salt from the bad
Weather that we've been getting.
Some little birds fly around just looking
For what little food they can scavenge
From the ground to feed themselves.
The lawn is all brown and the grass is all
Dead from the cold winter weather too.
The neighbor's hedge is busy with all of
The birds trying to find a place with some
Warmth. The squirrels and rabbits are
Foraging for some food as well, as they
Know that we have a long road ahead
Until Spring will finally get here several
Months from now. The gray sky looks
Like it is just waiting for Spring to get
Here so it can help the world with some
Warm weather so it can help the plants
To bloom and flourish once again, while
I just sit here and pray for the sun and
Spring to get here sooner than later.

When I get to the point where I just can't take
Anymore...I do as I always do and turn to my
Friend... to my sea of sanctuary. There goes
My tightness of chest and taught forehead as I
Ease back and swim in the sea, my sea of
Sanctuary. Her waves release all my stressors
And upset as she leads me on in her continuous
Motion of waves. SomeTymes at the seashore
I just stand and stare at her in all of her power
And magnificence as she goes on from shore to
Shore to shore. She moves with the power of
The moon's gravity as she ebbs twice a day.
She effervesces as the tides come in and I
Drift along in myself wondering why everyone
Can't share in the peace and joy of her beauty
She gives so freely of herself. Her salty breath
Floats on as she crosses over the shoreline that
Spans over three quarters of our planet Earth.
The most wondrous sound of all of her sounds
Is as she breaks upon the myriad shores of my
Mind and soul. Her gifts relax me so I can move
On and take on the world one last Tyme... if not
Now, for forever more.

Aimee had been missing since Saturday night.
I missed her snuggling with me so I looked
Through the living room to no avail. I looked
Under the couch where she likes to play...No
Aimee. I looked in the dining room but she
Wasn't there either. I searched the bathroom,
Nope. I looked in my bedroom where she
Where she Loves to hide in a corner of my
Room under the pile of clothes. She would
Spend much of her day sleeping, but still no
Aimee. I was beginning to get worried by
Now because she Loves to sleep all day until
Around seven or eight o'clock and I knew
She always shows up then. Still... no Aimee.
I went to the hall and asked Rich if he had seen
Her. No, no go there either. The only other
Place she likes to hide is in the basement. So
I turned on the light and saw her there at the
Bottom of the stairs. I called to her, but she
Didn't move. I called to her again and still no
Movement, so I walked carefully down the
Stairs calling out to her. When I got to the
Bottom of the stairs I could see that there was
No movement at all. I thought she may have
Fallen and hurt herself, but this wasn't the case.
As I touched her, I could feel instantly that she
Was cold and stiff. I realized then that she had
Passed on someTyme in the last day or so. I
Felt my eyes well up as I began to cry for the
Loss of a great pet and friend. Aimee was one
Of the best pets I had ever owned and she will
Be greatly missed and never forgotten. It's
Hard to lose such a good friend at such a young
Age. She was only six years old.

Alive

You make me feel alive. You make me
Feel renewed and fresh. There's nothing
That can make me Love you even more
Than I already do. You are my Lover
And you are my best friend. Somewhere
In the middle I find hope again to keep
On trying even though I am feeling down
And depressed today. Your Love is like
A nice warm blanket on a cool, cool night:
Soft, cozy and comfortable. When I get
To hold you it is like a pair of friends all
Wrapped around me and enveloping me
Me in Love. The only thing better is to
Get to kiss you. It truly is the best feeling
In the universe. It is a wonderful feeling
That only you can give to me, it is the best
Way to make a perfect ending to my day.

Auntie Jeanne

She was always my favorite Aunt that I had
Growing up. We were very close, in fact
She always felt like my second mom most
Of the Tyme. She was always letting my
Cousins, my sister and I play together. We
Were like one big happy family that way.
She always had the best stories to tell us
When we got together. She was also known
For taking us to the Swan Lake Boat Club.
My older cousin Laurie would baby sit us
When we were younger. Auntie Jeanne was
The best cook in town. We never had lots
Of money, but we were sure rich in Love
And caring. I know to this day we don't
See as much of her as we used to as when
We were young, but we always pick up
Right where we left off. I do so miss her
Pancakes in the mornings on weekends
When my sister and I would stay over night
At her house. Some people get older while
They are younger, still she looks the same
Today as she did back then when we were
Kids. I Love and miss her to death. We
Were close as children, we are ever closer
To this day. No, she never gets older, she
Just gets better.

Black and Blue

Hey little sister, you know that it's true,
You'll always be black and I'll always be blue.
Your color stands stark as any a hue,
You'll always be black and I'll always be blue.
Hey little sister, you know that it's true,
I'll always be there and I'll always Love you,
You'll always be black and I'll always be blue.
Hey little sister tell me what's new,
I know just how you feel, I've been there too,
You'll always be black and I'll always be blue.
These colors mean something these colors are true,
You'll always be black and I'll always be blue.

Blue Again

The skies above are blue again
And all the trees are growing green,
Summer is finally here once more
In all of the things we do and see.

Birds are busy nesting
Making room for all that's new,
The sunshine seems to go on forever,
It brings me up when I'm feeling so blue.

I go out for a little walk
Just to breathe in the fresh air,
I look at all the flowers
And a nest of rabbits resting there.

I go outside just to see the lawn
I feel the grass between my toes,
It's a soft and very lush world of green
In everywhere that it grows.

I Love to feel the sunshine
As she warms us with all of her rays.
And at night the moon will rise above,
With his bright face that he'll amaze.

Blue Today

I'm feeling sad and blue today
I wish I didn't feel this way.
For now I must get through these blues
This is not the kind of life I choose.
Maybe again when the sun does shine
I'll be feeling better and feeling fine.
I feel like a puppet without any strings
Or like a bird with broken wings.
Feeling so low can make me cry
When I get so low I wish I'd die.
Maybe I should go back to bed
To cure the upset in my head.
Because when I go to bed and sleep
I'll fall into nice dreams so deep.
My day is cloudy and soon it will rain
Perhaps it will wash away my pain.
And finally after my "storm" does end
My broken mind and heart will mend.

Bucket of Frogs

One day, when it was warm and sunny on a
Summer's day, my sister and I would go to
The gully and play around by the pond there.
Now, for whatever reason eludes me, there
Was a fire that was burning on the other side
Of the park where we would play baseball.
As it was, the pond was just brimming with
Hundreds and hundreds of frogs. There were
Some kids that were being mean and nasty
To the frogs and throwing them into the fire
To watch them burn and then pop like a
Firecracker when they exploded. I was so
Mad at those kids, but I couldn't do anything
To make them stop what they were doing.
My little sister freaked out at the disgust of
It all and ran back home and got a big bucket.
She spent the next several hours catching all
Of the frogs and toads that she could fit into
The bucket. We went home to take the frogs
Away from those kids. My mom saw the big
Bucket of frogs and told us there was no way
That we were going to turn them all loose in
Our yard. So what did we do? We took the
Big bucket of frogs back to the gully and put
Them all back in the pond and hoped that they
Would be safe from those mean kids. I can
Remember not sleeping for several days just
Worrying about those frogs and toads. It was
Truly traumatic to my ten year old mind that
People could be so mean and cruel to destroy
Other living things, especially some helpless
Little frogs and animals.

Bumpy Road Ahead

The world is spinning all around me
And I'm down in a hole just trying
To keep myself from suffocating.
The hole is so black and never warm.
It is so starkly dark that there's no
Light to be found, just black on black
On black to it's three dimensions.
There's nary a bit of light from around
It's edges to the outside world. It's
Just cold and dank and dark and never
Ever do you feel peace or at ease as
The black hole that you're in doesn't
Allow for visitors to reach in to provide
You with some help. All those that really
Know you, know that you've got to
Fight for your breath for every second
That you're in this Hell. When you get
A chance to hold onto it's slippery slope
You just stay there focused on surviving
And it's every man for himself. Grab on
To whatever you can for the bumpy road
Ahead is just beginning. Hold onto any
Thing that you can. The cold black tomb
You're in is ready to close with you inside
And without anyone getting out alive.
No there's no way out alive, but then no
One ever thought you'd make it out alive
And kicking. So hold on, it's a bumpy
Road ahead.

Burning Bridges

"Don't burn bridges is what you told me…
You never know when you
May need it in the future."
So I processed it just that way.
I told myself not to say anything
No, I won't burn that bridge
Unless I have to.
And so it went on like that
For years and years.
But something went and changed all that…
You…You changed it
And you changed my life…
And NOT for the better either.
So what did I do?
I told the truth!!
And in the process
Did I burn a bridge with You?
Are you really kidding me?
You can't burn a bridge
That was never built in the first place.
No, I didn't burn a bridge with you…
You can't burn a bridge that never existed…
That doesn't exist…
That doesn't exist…
IT NEVER EXISTED!!

Childhood Friends

When you are young, you can make friends
So easily. That's not the same as you get to
Be older. You tend to be more picky and you
Get wrapped up in the everyday situations
That you now spend with your soul mate.
When I was younger the two things that I
Looked forward to were Summer vacation
And the County Fair. My childhood was
Rich with the wonderful things that you could
Do. We always spent Tyme with the neighbors
At the beaches in Portage, Wisconsin. We
Spent the hours making up games and playing
Games like kickball and baseball on our
Vacation Tyme. Those friends have all grown
Up and moved on with their lives. I wonder
If they remember the great Tymes we had as
We grew up together. I miss my childhood
Friends, as they were some of the nicest
People I have ever had the privilege of meeting.
Tymes change, people get older, but one thing
Is for certain: the friends that we had when we
Were young can never be replaced or forgotten.

Cling to Your Friends

The world's gone crazy
This world's gone mad,
It makes me feel nervous,
It makes me feel sad.

There's violence in the air
There's violence in the streets,
So you better be careful
Of the strangers that you meet.

If it comes down to a fight
You better not come out swinging
Because you never know
What weapons they're bringing.

And if you disagree
Don't be anybody's fool,
You might wind up dead
So you better play it cool.

No, nobody knows
Just where this could end,
So be as cool as you can
And cling to your friends.

For oh, so long my life was nothing but a
World of gray, devoid of all colors. Just
Shades and shades of gray over and over
Again. But then something marvelous
Happened. Little by little you started
Adding color to the palette and then you
Added the colors of me and you. Sure
We looked good but the rest of the world
Was still stark and gray. But like the artist
That you are, you just started adding strokes
Of color to the rest of the world around us.
You just took the canvas and added dabs
Of color here and dabs of color there until
The masterpiece was finally completed.
With bright, strong beautiful colors all
Around the world is now a rainbow of
Colors that are out there and everywhere
For everyone to see and enjoy.

Day After Day

All alone, someTymes she cries as she revisits
The haunts from her past as vivid as the day
That they happened to her. She cries alone
SomeTymes for no reason other than she's
Feeling sad again and again. She wishes that
Things could be different, but they aren't any
Different, they just stay the same. Moment
By moment she loses touch with reality, just
Crying for those who can't help themselves,
Crying for the lost souls in the world. Her
Eyes well up when she realizes that she can't
Do anything to change all the misguided ones like herself.
She is the reason that she is unhappy because
Of the fear she has of the unknown. Medications
Can't stop the problem, but they can change
The way that she views the unrest and pain
All around the world and herself as well. She
Refuses to take any medicines that could help
To make her life easier to take on each day.
She doesn't want to go through any of the
Side effects that she might or might not get.
She cries and cries again until she is worn
Out and the day comes to an end. She will
Have to face the world alone because of her
Ridiculous fears, as everyone knows that you
Won't have all of the side effects, but you
May have to decide if you can live with the
Help they will give you to take on your day
After day, or go it alone.

Down in a Hole

SomeTymes all I do is cry,
SomeTymes I wish I knew just why
I'm stuck here with a feeble brain
And all it does is cause me pain.
They say that I've got the blues,
I guess I've got to pay my dues.
SomeTymes I just feel all alone
It leaves my saddened to the bone.
So I just take another pill
To help stop me from being ill.
But the sadness isn't gone for long
My life's become a tragic song.
SomeTymes I feel so low and bad
I'm sitting here just feeling sad.
So I turn my faith to God above
And hope he'll send me down some Love.
I hope he'll stop the way I feel
My life seems so lost and so surreal.
I wish I wasn't born this way
I guess there's not much left to say
But there's one thing of which I'm sure
Someday they'll find a real cure.
And then I'll be feeling so darn great
I hope there isn't too much longer to wait.

Dream Tyme

Some dreams cam be prophetic
Some dreams will tell you lies,
I only know that when I'm sleeping
I want to dream of you all night.
Some dreams can be quite silly
You'll wake up laughing to yourself,
Some dreams can be quite scary
Some dreams can be a living hell.
Some dreams can make you happy
Some dreams can make you sad,
And when you wake up from dreams
You're left feeling oh, so mad.
Some dreams we dream in color
Some dreams are black and white,
Some dreams you feeling speechless
Some dreams will fill you full of fright.
Some dreams are hard to understand
In some dreams you hear a song,
I only know that when they're over
Some dreams make you want to sing along.
Some dreams seem to go on forever
In some dreams you see the dead,
Some dreams make new connections
To those we miss inside our head.
Some dreams are really strange
In some dreams you see your friends,
In some dreams we relive good memories
I hope these dreams will never end.

Dreams

I wish I knew what my dreams mean. They
Are someTymes pleasant, often intense, and
They have been known to be extremely scary.
They seem to be extensions of situations that
Occur from Tyme to Tyme in my life. They
Often leave me scared half to death. When I
Wake up, it is someTymes hard to get back to
Sleep, because they seem so real. Some people
Say that you can control your dreams, but I have
Never gotten control of my dreamscapes. It
Would be great if I could. I often have dreams
That I'd like to remember, but when I wake up
In the morning I can't remember them at all.
SomeTymes I write them down in a notebook
So I can keep a record of them. They seem so
Intense that I write them down and want to
Remember them later, but usually all I can
Get is the memory or two from my notes,
Even though they were so clear in my mind
When I wrote them down.

Earthbound

SomeTymes I feel so low
That I must look up to see down,
I'm so lost and feeling sad
As I watch the world go around,
And everyone can tell
By the look upon my face,
I'm so way out of sorts
I'm in a Tyme without a place,
And it is at this Tyme
Where I just paint on a smile,
So people think I'm fine
It's been that way now for a while,
I need some real good friends
And I need the kind that
Will be there till my end,
Now I am not sure why
I have to live this way,
I'm just stuck here lost in Tyme
Without a word to say,
Life is so despairing
All I seem to do is cry,
I'm so tired of being blue
I need some wings to fly,
And when my number comes up
I will not put up a fight,
I'm ready now for heaven
I'm ready now for flight,
Now I will be so quiet
When I reach for heaven's door,
I'm finally ready to enter
I am not earthbound anymore.

Faith

We used to be the best of friends and spend
All of our free Tyme together. We were the
Kind of friends to always be there for one
Another, regardless of the situation. Nothing
Could come between us. We were so very
Close in so many, many ways. But then
Someone came between us and started to
Put a wedge between our friendship and has
Been trying to split up to minds that were
One and the same. It's been months since
I have seen your wonderful smiling face.
God knows just how very much I miss you
And all of the things that we would be doing.
Yet, somehow I know that this is just one
Obstacle that has cut off our relationship
That can be changed if you just put your
Mind to it. I know that you are a true
Friend and I know how much we mean to
One another. So now all I can do is just
Wait it out. Everyone knows that once
United we will not be divided by anything
Or anyone who would try to keep us apart.
Our connection to one another will always,
Always be there just waiting for a chance
To join up together sooner or later...I just
Need to have FAITH.

For Her Sake

Once there was a boy who looked like he
Was happy and go lucky young man like
So many other children, but he was very
Different from the others around him.
When he went to school, he felt like the
Others hated him because he was so smart.
He always knew all the answers that the
Teachers posed to the class, so many of
Them came to him for the answers.
What the other children didn't know was
That when he went home from school
His parents fought all of the Tyme and
Very rarely got along. This fighting that
Came between his parents made him sad.
So sad that he would often think about
Killing himself. He was very afraid that
His father would hurt his mother when they
Were fighting. He was very close with his
Mother and he was worried about her all
Of the Tyme. He often cried at the Tymes
His classmates were enjoying their lunch
Hours. He worried that something very bad
Would happen to her. But one day he realized
That he couldn't change his parents so he tried
To be the best kid in school so his parents
Would be proud of him. His mother was
Very proud of him and she told him that he
Brought her joy to her world. And from that
Day on he knew that he had to be strong for her
And he always was for her sake.

For Sue

While sitting in my great big chair
I heard a voice that wasn't there.
It came to me from my distant past
It's finally come to me at last.
And even though I'm here alone
I know I'll soon hear from your phone.
Or maybe we'll run into one another soon
Or be reminded of you as I hear one of our tunes.
We used to spend our free moments together
For 22 years through any kind of weather.
But someone's cut the cord that binds our Love
Yet I know that by the Lord above
We share a Love that is eternally strong
By my good friend Sue is where I belong.
One day soon we'll be close again
This Tyme we'll be forever friends.

Friends Till the End

Everywhere I go I know you'll be there
A friendship like ours is oh, so rare,
I like it when we're holding hands
Or taking a walk with our feet in the sand,
I like to sleep right next to you
It brings me up when I'm feeling blue,
When we go out I know just what you'll eat
Spending Tyme with you just can't be beat,
It's fun when we have over some guests
Just watching some movies can be the best,
When I'm with you I can be myself at last
And when we're together Tyme goes so fast,
When it gets cold, with you I'll cuddle
Even when you talk you're oh, so subtle,
You're the one I Love to hug and kiss
When you are gone you're the one I miss,
I'm so happy that you're in my life
When I'm upset you end my strife,
And when you're head is resting on me
There's no other place I'd rather be,
I know that you are my best friend
You're the one who'll be there till the end.

From Me to You

Everything in me that's good
I learned my Love, from you.
You have helped me in ways
That are yet to be revealed.
You taught me to be more quiet and reserved,
I had always been the life of the party
But you came along and helped me,
You helped me to restrain myself
And not always be so loud,
But to be more silent and in observance
As it is nice to be seen and not always heard.
Your smile and Love makes me realize
How very lucky I am
To have found you in this lifeTyme.
You always think of others before yourself.
Your demeanor is always at its best possible.
You are not just a friend,
You're my husband and soul mate.
You quite simply are
The best thing that has ever happened to me.

Get Through It

SomeTymes when I am feeling down and out,
I get to feeling like the depression that I am
In will never end. I seek to find a way out
Of the hole that I've fallen into. SomeTymes I can
Just listen to music to help ease my raw nerves.
More often that not, I turn to my friends and hope
That can help ease my pain and sorrow. There
Are Tymes that the only way out is to just have
A good cry and get it out of my system. When
The depression settles after a good amount of
Tyme, I can someTymes just sleep it off in a nap.
And when things get really rough I will sleep
It off over a period of days or even weeks.
These types of situations are the hardest to deal
With. It is no fun to sleep for days and or weeks
At a Tyme, but someTymes that is all you can
Do to get through it.

Getting Help

SomeTymes in life we get to a place where know
Someone who needs help, but we're not sure
How to go about helping that person find the
Right path that leads them back to sobriety
And back to health. Our first reaction is always
The same, we get stunned and go into shock
Because we can't believe that someone we
Know and care for has gotten themselves into
The mess that is heroin addiction. We want
To stand on the mountain and yell "What are
You doing…and why are you doing it?" We
Can get angry and yell and scream about it.
Yet it seems to do no good because it causes
The person involved to become angry and
Defensive. You can try the opposite reaction
And try to be a Loving guide as they watch
Their life coming apart. This does very little
To help the person get clean and sober. The
Only thing you can do is to let the person find
Their sobriety when they finally come to the
Conclusion that it is really up to them to take
That first step towards getting themselves
Clean and sober and then be a sounding board
To help them when that Tyme comes and they
Are ready for help and then offer them the
Help of getting their life back together.

Good Friends

I talked to you for the first Tyme in ages. I
Can't remember why it had been so long.
I called to tell you that our favorite singer,
George Michael had passed away that day
On Christmas morning. You were busy, so
We didn't talk for long. We spoke a few
Days later and you were quite cordial. This
Tyme we spoke like we had years ago. It's
Always good to hear from you, but often it
Will leave me feeling out of sorts for a while
Afterwards. You told me that you and your
Boyfriend had broken up. It is always nice
To have someone special to share your Tyme
With. I had forgotten how attached you were
To your dog. It's just like me and my cats
Are I guess. You were thoughtful to share
With me over the loss of Aimee. I have often
Thought you should stop by and visit with
Rich and myself. We could play some music,
Watch a movie, play chess or cards. We're
Pretty versatile. It's nice to know that you are
Able to look back and realize we used to both
Really care a lot for one another and that we
Still do too. As I have often said, you can't
Have too many good friends. It is nice to
Know that you will be one of them.

Goodbye, George

This last year was a most difficult year.
We lost David Bowie, Prince, Chris Cornell
Chester Bennington and the one that I will
Miss the most is Mr. George Michael.
I have Loved his music from the word "go".
His vocals can reach into your heart and
Fill it will soul. He literally had the voice
Of an angel.
He could make you feel Loved
With just his words.
He changed pop music history forever.
He could get you up on your feet and dance
Or he could slow the moment down
And move your heart.
His looks were always the cutting edge
As he brought his style and handsomeness
To the forefront of the '80's, 90's and beyond.
To this day, his iconic trends set the standard
For men of all types: the five o'clock shadow,
The goatee and the Cesar.
His music has stood the test of Tyme
It is such a shame that he didn't get a chance
To leave us more of his music to enjoy.
He will be greatly, and sorely missed.

Goodbye My Love

Goodbye my Love its hard to say goodbye
When I feel like I shouldn't be alive
I feel I should have been the one to die
Its so hard to say goodbye.

You were my constant companion
For nine long years you were next to me
I'm so sorry now that you are gone
I miss the way you Loved to sit with me.

You Loved just laying in the sun
You touched my life in so many ways
You are the one I Loved so much
I don't know why God took you away.

You had lost your health and drive
Oh, my Love its so hard to die
When there's no sun up in the sky
I hoped you'd understand just why,

I had to let him put you to your final rest
Where you are now finally and totally free
I still feel you next to me
Please let me say goodbye and finally leave.

Oh, my Love its hard to say goodbye
When there's no sun up in the sky
You were the lucky one to get to die
There's no Love left in the world for me to try

Goodbye...Goodbye...Goodbye
    Good bye...Goodbye
        Goodbye.

Grandma Nitz

One of my fondest memories is one that I have
That goes back to the seventies. It is that of
My Great Grandmother, Grandma Nitz. She
Only lived a couple of blocks away from our
House on East Howard Street. I would take
Our lawnmower down the alley and mow her
Lawn for her. I remember that she had two
Pianos and several record players. One Tyme
When Dana and I were at her house she
Would play some hymns for us. She could
Really play the piano. The other thing she
Had was a huge collection of buttons that
She had probably saved for many years of
Her life. We would just sit and spend hours
Looking at the buttons and she would play
Her piano and we would sing along to if we
Knew the song. There's nothing that I wouldn't
Give to get another chance to sit and look
At all those buttons with my Great Grandma
Again and hear those old records that she
Used to play on her Victrola while we just
Sang along.

Great Grandma Nitz #2

She was a most wonderful character. She
Lived by herself in a little house not far
From us. She had the most wonderful
Antiques. She had several Victrolas and
Pianos and an organ. I used to Love to
Go to her house because she had a huge
Collection of buttons that were very old
And mysterious to me. All sizes and all
Shapes of many different colors too. She
Would always get her piano going and
She would sing all of the songs she knew
So well from church on Sundays. When
She got very excited, her voice would
Warble a bit off key, but that didn't matter
To me. We Loved her whether she sang
On key or not. One of my favorite things
To look at was her cases of rings that she
Sold for a dollar. Once in a while she would
Say, "Pick out one that fits you." so I'd
Try all of them on. Most of them were too
Big, but every once in a while I could find
One that fit me just right. She would say,
"You can pay me back when you make
You first million.". She was so thoughtful
That way. I especially looked forward to
The Christmas season because she would
Make her famous fruitcakes. She gave one
To all of the relatives as a gift. I can still
Remember how good they are and what
A great treat they made.

Hard to Tell

When you're not here,
Nothing's right, as hard as I try, try, try.
I can't seem to understand just why, why, why.
Everything that seemed so right, right, right
All came out all wrong, wrong, so very wrong.
I try as hard as I can, to make you happy
Yet, as still as hard as I try,
I can't keep up with the good deeds that you do
So often and so well.
I am but a simple man who only means you
So well, well, well.
I guess it's just me,
Sometimes its hard to tell, tell, tell.
So just do what can I say
I've said all that I can, can, can.
I guess I'll shut my mouth
And start listening again, again, and again.

Once there was a Tyme when I was oh, so brave
Never thinking about the future. Life was just a
Game I played for fun. Then you came into my
Life and everything changed around. I stopped
Running away from myself. I knew that when I met
You it was for good this Tyme. That scared me so
Much. How much you'll never know. All I ever
Wanted was you. Then I finally realized I had
To make some changes in the way I was living.
I knew the changes never come quickly, but when
They do come, they come swiftly. You brought
Out the best in me. This was something that I
Never thought possible before, let alone to be
Achievable. If there's one thing that I'd like you
To remember and that is that I give you all the
Love I have to give anyone, here and now. I
Promise you all of my life, then and now and
Here. You are the one that makes my life livable
And attainable. Thank you for all of that you give.
I know you will be here now and forevermore.

In Need of a Friend

When the day is shown gray
And I'm feeling so blue,
There's nothing much to say
And there's nothing more to do.

It's still winter outside
And it's feeling so cold,
I just can't deny that
I'm just feeling so old.

When my body's all achy
And I'm feeling so bad,
Who knows why again
Why I'm feeling so sad.

So cuddle up close
As I begin to cry,
I'm just not sure why
That I wish I would die.

And when the day is over
And the day comes to an end,
I'm still sitting here lonely
And in need of a friend.

In the Morning Light

When I wake up in the morning light
I can feel you're arms around me so tight,
I like to see you're handsome face
You have a smile I can't erase,
I Love the way you're such a good cook
You can bring me up with just one look,
When I'm alone you're the one I crave
You're not only strong you're also quite brave,
You can bring me up when I'm feeling blue
I just want to spend my whole life with you,
Some Tymes we sit and do nothing but talk
While other Tymes we'll just go for a walk,
Of the people I know, you're my best friend
Spending Tyme with you helps my mind to mend,
I like the way you rest your head on me
Right by your side is where I long to be,
In everything we do we always share
Together we make such a wonderful pair,
I Love the way you hold me so strong
In your arms is where I belong.

Don't change for me
Don't change a thing,
I Love you for the Zen you bring.
You are smart and you are wise,
Your Love is where my future lies.
And when I see your handsome smile
My heart beats fast for just a little while.
And when I look into those eyes of brown
They bring me up when I'm feeling down.
You're so gentle and so very kind
You have such a beautiful mind.
You'll always be my closest friend
You're the one I'll Love until the end.
I admire you for the Love you bring
You're Love makes life eternally Spring.
You make me laugh because you're funny
You take dark days and make them sunny.
You'll always be my special Love
You're my gift from God above.
I'm so happy when I'm in your arms
You complete me with your stately charms.
You've helped me conquer all of my fears
I Love you so very much my dear,
Whether you're near or whether you're far
I Love you just the way you are.

Keep On Trying

There are days when depression pulls you down
Those days you get lost inside your head,
On those days you feel so lonely
On those days you wish that you were dead.
It's important to take your medications
Some days you get tired of taking your pills,
SomeTymes it feels like they're not working
And they're not overriding your ills.
There are so many medications
You may need to try more than one kind,
Some can work better than others
Some meds can play tricks within your mind.
You need to take your medications regularly
You must find the right combination,
When your medications don't work out
It can lead to aggravation.
Some days are harder than others
To get things right you need therapy too,
Meds and therapy work together
But some days you just can't shake the blues.
Some days you wish you weren't alive
It seems like things never change,
But if you keep on trying
You will yourself begin to rearrange.

Let the Pain Out

Today is a day I'm feeling so blue
I don't know why, but I just do,
I see my therapist and I take my meds
I take them at night when I go to bed,
I don't know why I just want to cry
SomeTymes I wish that I would die,
I don't have very much to say
I wish I didn't feel this way,
SomeTymes I wish I'd never been born
I'm so upset and my feelings are torn,
I wish I didn't have this brain
'Cause it's no fun to be insane,
I live some days up and others down
I miss my friends when they're not around,
My moods change as often as the weather
I hope some day I'll be feeling better,
SomeTymes I want to scream and shout
And let all of this pain all out,
I hope some day they'll find a cure
Until that Tyme, my life's a blur,
Maybe in the future my mind will be free
Living without depression's how I want to be.

Lights Out!

Over the years, I have always had trouble
Falling asleep. When I am in a manic mode
Nothing seems to help me to fall into sleep.
Then I discovered a new way to pass the
Tyme until I finally do. I call it "Lights Out."
What I do is to have my stereo play me some
Very relaxing music with the lights out. I have
Learned that by having the music play when
All the lights are out, you can hear the music
In a different way. I find that when the lights
Are all out, you actually hear the music in a
New way, because you will hear parts of it
That you choose you don't normally hear when
You are listening to it with them on. When the
Lights are off, you have no point of focus in the
Room, so all you do is listen and try to put a
Picture to the sounds that you are now hearing
For the first Tyme in this way. I have always
Enjoyed music, but this is a great way to pass
The Tyme till you finally get to sleep. When
You can't sleep, this can be more than very
Frustrating to say the least. I have always
Heard that counting sheep will help you to fall
Asleep. This has never worked for me, but
Listening to very slow, calming relaxing music can
Help you pass the Tyme without the lights may
Be just the trick you need.

Little Bird

A little bird came to my window
He wanted to sing a song,
I was surprised and somewhat happy
I hoped he'd let me sing along.
It was a song for spring Tyme
It was a tale he knew so well,
It was a song about the mating season
It was a story he liked to tell.
So he sang about the good Tymes
And then he sang about the sad,
He liked to sing about his brood,
They were the best Tymes he'd ever had.
After he was finished he turned and flew away
Then I began to feel so blue,
I've got his song inside my head now
So I will sing his song to you.

Lost and Down

It's another day I'm feeling lost and down
And on my face you'll find a frown.
I'm sick and tired of feeling sad
And even more tired of feeling bad.
Some days I'm feeling just so tired
While other days I'm way too wired.
What I've got they call the blues
I'm tired of living in these shoes.
SomeTymes all my head does is ache
SomeTymes it's too much for me to take.
So I call a friend up on the phone
To help me feel not so all alone.
So I turn to God to find some peace
I hope I'm not far out of his reach.
SomeTymes it's hard to make it through my day
I guess there's not much left for me to say
So I'll take my meds and go to bed
Perhaps I'll find some peace when I am dead.

Love is Forever

When life goes wrong
And nothing is right,
I turn away from the cold
And steer to the light.
I seek your attention
I look for you Love,
In the form of an angel
God sent from above.
So take my hand
And hold it now,
Make a wish for Love
As we make our vows.
Love takes a life
And gives it bliss,
It all starts
In the form of a kiss.
You are my Love
You are my friend,
Our Love is so strong
And never will end.
Yes, our Love grows strong
With the passage of Tyme
I'll always be yours
And you'll always be mine.
They say Love is forever
They say Love is kind,
We will always be together
Until the end of Tyme.

Milwaukee

I have spent the last thirty years or so living
In the city of Milwaukee, Wisconsin. It just
Happens to be the largest city in the state of
Wisconsin. The nice thing about living in a
Big city is that you can be almost invisible in
A big city, especially if you like to have your
Privacy and not have everybody knowing all
Of your business by just staying to yourself
And avoiding others. One of the nice things
About living in a big city like Milwaukee is
That there is always something going on if
You really enjoy being busy. There's are so
Many church festivals and ethnic festivals
Going on all during the summer months.
There are lots and lots of places to go to
Shop or go out to eat. There are always so
Many sporting events and places to go year
Round if you happen to be a sports aficionado.
There are some down sides to living in a big
City. You can spend years in a neighborhood
And never get to know and trust anyone there.
The other bad thing about living in a big city
Is that with more people, there is more crime
Going on. This is a very big problem for me.
There's definitely something to be said about
Being in a place where you feel safe and secure
All of the Tyme. I never really feel safe here,
As there's always a problem with crime in
Milwaukee.

Miss Kaydee

She has eyes that sparkle with the color green
She has the brightest eyes you've ever seen
She has a nose that is dark, cold and wet
She has the nicest demeanor I've ever met
She has teeth that are sharp, her claws are too
She brings me up when I'm feeling blue
She lays with me when I go to sleep
She goes down to the cellar where she Loves to creep
She goes on safari to catch a mouse
She likes to think she runs the house
She has long legs that are lithe and thin
She leaves paw prints wherever she's been
She likes to sit and watch T.V.
She is ever so placid when she sits with me
She moves so quick without a sound
She is the nicest cat to have around
She is the prettiest cat in the whole wide world
She is may favorite cat, she's my Kaydee girl.

Miss You Much

I miss you so much
Since you've been gone,
Everything that was right
Now feels so wrong.
You and I were so close
As close as can be,
So please come back
You're the one I need.
Friends like you
Don't come along very much,
I miss your smile,
And I miss your touch.
And if you're scared
To come back now,
I'll say it again
And I'll say it loud.
You're the one I Love
You're the friend that I need,
Please hear me now,
You're my Love in deed.
Don't ever doubt
The way that we feel,
Our Love is so right
Our Love is so real.
I've said it before
And I'll say it again,
You're the One I Love
You're my best of friends.

Mom

There are so many things that I am very thankful
For. But the one thing that comes first to mind
Is just how grateful I am to have such a great
Mother. She is someone who has always been
There for me my entire life. We have been
Through a lot together. Regardless of all of the
Circumstances, she is always supportive of me.
I try to be just as supportive to her as she has
Been for me. She is the one person in my
Family that I can always count on to be there
For me. Not only is she a great person, she is
Also a great support to all of the other people
Who count on her for so many, many things.
She is truly one of the kindest people I have
Ever known. She is a person who will tell it
To you just like it is…No beating around the
Bush with her. She always says just what is
On her mind, but it always is said in a kind
Way. She is always so kind and thoughtful to
Others and especially with those in her family.
She is also a very Loving person. I Love her
For all of the Love that she shares with myself
And others too. People always tell me that I
Am so very lucky to have such a great mother.
I just simply smile and tell them that I already
Know!

My Dearest Friend

When I feel your Love within my heart,
I'll give this life a brand new start.
I'm ready to give this world another chance,
As I find I'm filled with our romance.
I think of you throughout my day,
I think of all the things I want to say
To let you know that my Love is true,
My life began the day I met you.
You stole my heart when you took my hand,
I never knew that life could feel so grand.
I Love the things that you do for me,
I Love the way you set my soul free.
You make me so proud to be your Lover,
I Love you so much more than any other.
And when I look so deep in your eyes,
My soul is free to start to fly.
And when it seems I'm feeling down,
I only need you to come back around.
You start my heart afire with a kiss,
There's nothing better in life than this.
And if our world should come to an end,
I know I've spent my life with my dearest friend.

My Friend Sue

She was the best friend that I ever had
She could bring me up when I was feeling sad
She knew just the right words to say
She was so helpful in every way
She knew just the right thing to calm me down
She could speak to me without making a sound
She liked good food and maybe some wine
She was just like an angel, she was divine
She was as close to perfect as she could be
She could always finish my sentences for me
She knew that we'd be friends for life
She could have been my perfect wife
She knew that I would always be there for her too
She would call on me when she was feeling blue
She knew that I was her closest friend
She knew that I'd be there for her till the end
She had the prettiest smile I've ever seen
She was always so kind and never mean
She was always close by, we'll never part
She was a little woman with a great big heart.

My Heart and Soul

I Love you with all of my heart and soul.
You have helped me make it through
Many a situation that turned out to be
The wrong decision for me. You are so
Very handsome and strong. You help
Me to keep my focus on the road ahead
And not to get sidetracked with things
That aren't good for me. You are my
Rock that keeps me on the straight and
Narrow and you keep me happy, and I
Love you for that. You are the one who
Keeps me happy and safe. You are my
Support system and you keep constantly
Reminding me just how important it is
To stay on the road that I am treading on.
You are my hero. You guide me and Love
Me for being the person that I already am.
Thank you for helping me to always stand
Strong and tall. You will always be the one
That I Love.

I will always Love you for all of the kind
Things that you do for not only me, but
For others as well. I know that you are
A very giving person because that is just
The way you are. If there's one thing that
I could do to let you know much you
Mean to me, it would be to tell you that
You are my whole world and beyond.
You do things out of the compassion in
Your heart. In a world that grows so
Considerably colder as Tyme passes, it
Is nice to know that there are still people
Who are so kind, giving and supportive.
Your Loving ways show me that chivalry
Is not dead but so very much alive in all
Of the things that you are and do. Some
Tymes the simplest of things you do can
Mean so very, very much. Whether it is
Just holding hands or going for a little
Walk with you that I so very much enjoy
And appreciate. When you hold me in
Your arms and tell me how much you
Love me, I couldn't be happier or prouder
To have you in my life that completes me.
True Love is so rare and so hard to find,
But when you really find Love, you need
To hold on tight and never, ever let go.

Next Tyme Around

You put a gun up to my head
You made me wish that I was dead,
You liked to yell and scream at me
Is this the way life's supposed to be?
I was your mental punching bag
A life like this is such a drag,
You liked to drink your life away
I wish I could've make you change,
You liked to hurt me through and through
Is this what a dad's supposed to do?
We hadn't seen each other in such a long Tyme
I just wanted things to be all fine,
You were a great guy when you were sober
Because of how you lived your life is over,
On the day that you had died
A piece of me died deep inside,
I think of you on Father's Day
As I now wish my life away,
A father's supposed to Love his son
And not threaten him with a gun,
I hope one day we'll meet up again
Maybe this Tyme we'll be better friends.

Nightmare World

SomeTymes you wake up having nightmares
They can scare you in the night,
Some nightmares can be so horrifying
They can fill your heart with fright.
SomeTymes you have the same old nightmares
You can dream that your teeth are falling out,
And when you go and yell for someone
You can scream and nothing comes out.
SomeTymes you can dream you're drowning
And there's sharks swimming there too,
When you scream the water fills your lungs
You're better off swimming in pools.
SomeTymes you dream that you're falling
You can dream you're falling from the sky,
You fall and fall so rapidly
It makes you wish that you could fly.
SomeTymes you can dream that you're all alone
Or that you're in pit that's full of snakes,
Then all at once they attack and bite
These kind of dreams can give you the shakes.
SomeTymes you dream you're back at school
And you forgot to study for the test,
You can dream you don't know the answers
These dreams will fill you with unrest.

When I was a child I was so afraid of the dark.
This was because I used to watch horror movies
All the Tyme. I was mesmerized by those films
Of vampires, werewolves, monsters and so forth.
I never felt scared watching them, but they sure
Left a bad aftertaste in my mouth if you know
What I mean. The funny part was that I was not
Scared of the monsters themselves, I was scared
Of the movies where they were really violent
Towards other people. These kind of movies
Scared me to the bone. I Loved getting scared
As a child, but not by those true to life crime
Stories that could really happen to you. Those
Were the kind of thing you hear about or
Read about on the news. I once saw a movie
That scared me to death. I was never the same
After I saw that film. I was so scared that I had
Nightmares from it for years afterwards. I could
Remember waking up the entire family screaming
At the top of my lungs on many, many occasions.
Those movies were meant for adults, not children.
Need we ask why that is? Violence is not good
For children to see at any age, especially when
They are young and impressionable.

Off to Sleep

I want to eat you for breakfast,
I want to drink you in
Because you taste so fine.
I will never deny that I Love you
I Love You,
I LOVE YOU!
I want to Love you on a stellar plane
Because you know how to Love me so right.
I get lost in Love every moment
That you are here with me.
Hold me tightly my wonderful friend,
Hold me tighter than you ever have before.
When you have finally Loved me
Till the end of the night
I hope you will kiss me softly
As I fall off to sleep.

On Sunday

Sunday is the laziest day of the week. People
Usually sleep in later than most other days.
When we get up we have the wonderful
Chore of doing the weeks laundry and then clean
Up the place and finishing projects that we have
Begun and not completed during the week. On
Sunday is the day for soft music and getting caught
Up on the news that we have missed during the
Week. The nice thing about Sunday is that you
Can take things nice and easy. There's no reason
To rush to get everything done right away. You
Can just relax and do things at a slower pace.
Even eating is on a help yourself schedule on
Sundays. You eat when you get around to it.
There's no set Tyme for lunch and dinner on the
Weekend, especially on Sunday. You eat when
You get around to it. So just relax and enjoy
The slowest day of the week.

One Little Kiss

When you're not here
I feel so alone,
It's like I'm not alive
Whenever you're gone.
When I make my way
Through a lonely day,
I wish you'd come back
I wish that you'd stay.
Life's not right
When you're not in it,
I wish you were here
I'd take you back in a minute.
Hold me, hold me
You're my angel of Love
You're my guiding light
That God sent from above.
For when you feel lonely
And you can no longer fly,
I'll be your angel
Who'll lift you so high.
So please come back
And give me back my bliss,
It all starts
With one little kiss.

Our True Love

You…You're the one,
You're the one I Love,
Above…Above all others,
You're the One that I live for,
Now…Now and for all of Tyme,
Yours and Mine…Two hearts, two hearts,
Two hearts that beat as One.

Me…and You in Love,
Just Me and You in Love,
For as long as we both shall live,
For as Long as…
For as Long as we both shall live.

Our true Love,
It will rise above,
It will rise above,
It will rise above all others.

I will share my Love with You,
For now…For now…for now and for all of Tyme,
My one…
My one…
My one true Love of my life…
I will share…I will share…I will share my life
And my Love with You.

Pain

Pain…it is a word that I know so well. It's
Something that I have lived with for years
And years. It is something that I have learned
To hide and conceal. When people ask me
How I'm doing I just smile and put on a
Happy face to cover up the reality of how
I'm really doing as people don't want to really
About negative things anyway. People will
Always say that they are concerned and ask
What they can do to help. Well the truth is
Nothing. I can't change the chemistry of my
Brain, so I just keep taking my pills and my
Medicines that don't fix the problem, but
Make it tolerable enough to live with. Pain
And sorrow are my two constant reminders
Of what it is like to live with bipolar disease.
Pain can be a headache, it can be an achy
Body that hurts so much it makes me want
To throw up. It's not a typical headache or
Body ache. It is totally excruciating pain that
I wish wasn't there and I wish would just go
Away. Unfortunately I can't change the way
That I feel so I have learned to just not talk
About it and keep my mouth shut.

Play Tyme

When I was just a little boy
Playing filled my life with joy,
We'd play in the park for hours
Building sand castles and towers,
We'd play kickball with my friends
The days seemed to have no end,
We'd ride high up on the swings
Just pretending we had wings,
We'd soar up in the sky
Pretending we could fly,
We'd swim in the lake all day
Just to pass the Tyme away,
We liked skateboarding down the hills
It gave us all a thrill,
We'd go riding through the town on our bikes
SomeTymes we'd just go on long hikes,
We'd climb up high in the trees
Just to catch a breeze,
We always played till the dark set in
The next day we'd do it all over again.

Portage

I grew up in the small town of Portage, Wisconsin.
It is a town of about ten thousand people. It is a
Town where everybody gets to know everyone
Pretty well. It is a town that is one where you get
To go to school with everybody's brothers, sisters
And family. It is a nice place to live in that there
Isn't a lot of crime and it is a place where you can
Know and trust your neighbors. I can remember
Going out of town on vacation and leaving our
Keys with the neighbors next door so they can
Keep an eye on your home and feed and take care
Of your pets. It'd nice to be able to trust those
People you live by and they can count on you to
Do the same. The only bad part about living in a
Small town is that you can't be anonymous and
Just blend into your surroundings because every
One knows everybody's business good and bad.
You can trust people because you know them so
Well. It sure is nice to know that if you need
Someone to keep an eye on your things or your
Home that they are there for you. You can get
To know people well and you can know what's
Going on all around you, if you just take the Tyme
To do so.

Rain

When all the winds and clouds collide
And they are filled with rain inside,
The water falls lightly to the ground
So soft and gentle without a sound.
They fill the ground with simplicity and ease,
SomeTymes they turn to snow and freeze.
Rain helps the crops to thrive and grow
And often a storm will sometimes blow
All the clouds around in space
Yet the drops dry without a trace.
Rain helps to wash our world so clean
Leaving all of the foliage lush and green.
Rain water flows down to the ocean
Where waves stir the sea with a gentle motion.
Rain falls to the earth from the heavens above
A precious gift from our God above.

Rain Storms

The other night I woke up in the middle
Of a very loud and intense rain storm.
I Love the sound of the rain and storms,
But this one was very intense and loud
And the lightening was so bright that it
Lit up the entire room. Usually I enjoy
The sound of rain and just close up the
Windows, but I was so scared I couldn't
Get back to sleep. When I finally did
Get back to sleep, I was awakened to
Find that I was awakened several more
Tymes that night by the loud sounds of
Thunder and lightening. I don't scare
Easily, but this storm was the exception
To the rule. I was sure that the walls
Were going to come apart from the wild
Winds. When I awoke up from the next
Morning I was pleasantly surprised to
Find everything was just fine. Thank
God for good architecture and support.

Rich is Always Right

I am the kind of person who doesn't like
To admit when I am wrong…especially
When I am completely sure about it or
Rather I think I'm 100% in the right…
So naturally you need to get someone's
Facts and opinions to back you up, you
Go with the obvious choice, by asking
My husband Rich to give you his thoughts
On the matter. And would you believe it,
I was in the wrong once more…and Rich
Is right like rain. Now, secretly I feel like
I am usually going to be right about that
Something and then I get the absolute
Truth of the matter tossed in my face by
Rich who, as I have said before is going
To be right 99.9% of the Tyme or more.
I have tried to correct him about the truth
Of things for years now. I always blurt
Out what I am thinking because I am
Sure that I am going to be right this Tyme
And I will not be wrong, but as sure as
Tomorrow will come and as sure as the
Day will end, I get the truth told to me
By Rich, who will go out of his way to
Point out that he is always right and that
I am in the wrong. Once again, I stand
Corrected.

So very many things come to mind when I
Think of my husband Richard. One of the
First things that I think of is how very, very
Loving that he is. Richard is the kind of
Person that will go out of his way to do
Things for others, even when he really
Would rather not do them. He is the one
Person who gives so much of his heart and
Soul into everything that he does. He will
Always put others' thoughts above his own.
He is really the nicest man that I have ever
Met. Even more important is the way he
Puts so much Tyme and consideration into
Everything that he does. He will do things
For others that he doesn't have to do, but
He does because of the great Love his
Parents have instilled in him. He always
Puts his family first, regardless of the
Circumstances. He gives so much of him-
Self to others that he puts their needs
Before his own. He is a very kind and
Generous person. He really enjoys being
Able to be there for others. I am so very
Lucky to have found the nicest man in the
World to be my husband. He truly is a
Person who enjoys making other people
Happy.

SomeTymes when you are happy in Love
And everything is going right, someone will
Throw a wrench into your system and try to
Mess everything up for you. Having said
That, it can be quite upsetting when it does
Happen. That's when you have to stand tall
And be very strong so as to avoid a problem
With the one that you Love. My advice is to
Be up front with both of the parties involved.
I am so happy to be the one who has common
Sense to be doing the right thing. I hope that
Someday as I look back upon the situation I
Can realize that I did the right thing by being
Strong and staying with the one that I Love
More than anyone else and that would be my
Husband Richard. We have been together now
Going on twenty three years and married now
Going on three years. I am so very lucky to
Have found real love in my lifeTyme. That
Is something to be very, very proud of.

Run to You

She walked back into my life
And changed what was wrong
And made it right.
With her soft, gentle words and wisdom.
She moved me to tears as I remembered
Our life once before.
As she is wise beyond her years,
She helped me face my fears
From long, long ago.
Her beauty and kindness are matched
Only by her intellect and strength
To hold me up when I'm feeing
So down…down…down
So very way, way down.
Like she has done for years gone by,
Her smile is a reminder of the good
Tymes we have shared over the years.
She tells me we have so many, many
More in the years to come.
Thank you for coming back into my life
And restoring my soul to where it once was.
Thank you for reminding me that
True Love never really goes away,
But lives on FOREVER.

Rusty Cage

Looking in the mirror I see a form of me
As I look I see I'm not just who I long to be,
Outside the world is moving, outside the world is strong
Still the outside world is a place I don't belong,
SomeTymes I feel so weak, someTymes I'm filled with rage
So I just stay here locked inside this rusty metal cage,
A cage that has no windows, a cage that has no doors
Just to see the sun outside leaves me here still wanting more,
A cage that's made so strong that I cannot get out
I'm feeing so trapped inside it makes me want to shout,
I'm so tired of being in here, so tired of being alone
I'm way too weary of being in this place I call my home,
So I stand here and I pace with nothing else to do
Because I'm still waiting for the grand return of you,
So until my Tyme is over, and until I'm finally free,
I will wait here all alone till you come back to me,

Sad Days and Bad Days

There are days when I feel quite lonely
Those days that you're not by my side,
Some days all you can do is cry a lot
When the day is over I'll be with you tonight.
Some days it's hard to get up and started
There are those days you can't get out of bed,
There are days that never go right
These days I can't get out of my head.
Sometimes depression rules over your day
There are those days when you can't shake it,
There are days when you feel like a low life
Those are the days that are hard to make it.
Bad days can creep on by without you
On those days you get stuck inside your mind,
Those are the days that you just make it through
On those days you wish you weren't alive.
Some days are hard to pull on by
On some days you can't shake the sadness,
Some days you need another's help
On those days you appreciate your gladness.
Some days you need to reach out to others
Or you need to call a friend on the phone,
Those are the days you want to go by fast,
On those days you do the best alone.

Sails Unfurled

Life is full of changes
To this you can't be weak,
You must exhibit all your strengths
To live life to it's peak.
When it's Tyme to make a stand
To do all that you can
And take on every challenge
It's Tyme to be a man.
To live life to it's fullest
Sometymes you must give in
But never give up the ship completely
And leave your sails a furl in the wind.
Living life can be quite painful
But it isn't out of reach
So be as brave as you can be
And practice what you preach.

Sam

She sits alone in a dog house…
Alone, yes alone every day as she waits
For her owners to take her to play, but
No one comes for her. Stillness and more
Stillness as she hopes that this will be the
Day that they want to play a game of fetch
With her. It's been so long since she has
Seen them around here. Once a day, some-
One comes to feed and water her. Still the
Rest of the day she just sits in stillness as
She waits for the day to come when she
Will be the one that they want to hang out
With and take her to the lake for a swim.
She remembers how much they used to
Spend Tyme with her on the weekends and
SomeTymes even during the day oh, so
Many years ago when she was just a pup
And her owners were younger too. "Oh,
Please come and play with me!" she begs.
"I want to get out of this cage and run, run
Run until I can't run anymore. I'd even
Sit good for a bath if it meant that you
Would spend a little Tyme with me today!"
But like the day began, it will end again
Where she just sits and waits alone, alone
Alone.

Shades of Blue

Everywhere I look, I'm looking for you,
But everything I see are only shades of blue.
And I'm looking for you in the stars,
The ones that shine on full true,
But all that I can see are lonely shades of blue.
I wander the streets,
Alone and without you,
But all that I can see
Are lonely shades of blue.
Shine on blue, shine on blue,
Shine on blue, shine on blue,
I'm shining bright blue for you.
And now as the end comes true,
I'm shining bright blue for you.
Burning blue, burning blue,
I'm burning bright blue for you.
I'm caught up in this haze
And there's nothing else I can do,
I'm burning bright blue, I'm burning bright blue,
I'm a fire that burns bright blue for you.

Snow Forts

In the winterTyme, our friends and I would
Always have a ball by making snow forts
In the back yard or at the park across the
Street from our house. We would spend
Hours just packing the snow and constructing
The walls of our forts. After they were strong
And sturdy, we would cover them in water
So they would freeze and be made of ice.
The neighbors and my sister and I never
Complained about the cold, not a bit. The
Bad part about making snow forts at the
Park was when we left them there, the older
Kids would always knock them down. We
Just made new ones out of the remnants
Of the old ones. Touché.

Snuggle Tyme

As I lay silently in thought, my cat Kaydee
Walked up next to me and began to meow
For some attention. I remember distinctly
Pulling her close to me to give her a kiss
And then she did the most amazing thing,
She sat herself down and began to snuggle
Up close to me and then she put her paw
Over her eyes to cover them and then she
Lay there all cuddled up next to me for
Some warmth and I felt she was also letting
Me know that she now trusts me completely
For the first Tyme in our cat/owner relationship.
I remember wondering why she chose now
To trust me to where she would snuggle up
Against me for the first Tyme. Now eight
Years into our friendship she trusts me. I
Have always wanted to have a pet that
Trusted me enough to sleep up next to me.
I've had ferrets, (not so friendly), and I
Have had several cats, but never one who
Would sleep next to me. It made me feel so
Proud that she now trusts me and hopefully
She will continue our snuggling Tyme when
She wants to take naps. Here's to great
Pet/owner relationships. The kind where
The pets trust their owner implicitly enough
To snuggle with them. Trust is an amazing
Thing that doesn't come standard in all
Relationships. It is something that is learned
As well as earned.

So Much to Give

SomeTymes it's hard to stay in my happy place
When I've got so much on my mind,
SomeTymes those old blues come creeping in
And those old blues can be so unkind.

They sure know how to drag you down
They can sure make you feel so low,
Because when those blues come back for more
Down is the only way left to go.

But sometimes those blues won't leave so easy
No, those blues won't leave like they should,
They just hang around and bring you down
And then you won't be left feeling so good.

So summon all your courage up
And send those blues on their way,
Remember there's always tomorrow
And it can be so much better that today.

So when the sun comes shining through my window
It can be a brand new day to live,
There's nothing but fresh air all around me
I know I've got so much more to give.

Some Days

Some days I just feel so lonely
Those days stuck inside my head,
Some days just drag on and on
On those days I wish that I was dead.
There are days when I am not alone
When there are people everywhere,
I can be surrounded but still lonely
I must reach out to those who care.
On days filled with depression
I wonder why God made me this way,
Still I keep taking all of my meds
Some day my depression will wash away.
SomeTymes depression goes on forever
I've been in therapy for years,
There are Tymes so overwhelming
I get lost inside my tears.
On days when it's so cloudy
The sky can look so gray,
These days seem to go on forever
I wish my sadness would go away.
There are days when I need to be all alone
On those days I feel so lost,
I close my eyes and pray softly
Losing my mind can be the cost.
Some days I wake up all depressed
On those days it's hard to sleep,
On those days I just cry and cry
On those days the Tyme just creeps.

Stop It!

"Stop it!"
"Stop it you're killing him!"
"You're killing my brother!" she cried out
As she watched her father choke
The throat of his slender neck.
But her father didn't stop,
He grabbed his head
And started pounding it
On the edge of the brass bed.
Over and over her father slammed
Her brother's head onto the bed...
Till finally she jumped on her father's back
And started hitting him as hard as she could.
Then he finally let go of me
As I just lay on the floor
Just struggling to catch my breath
Too worried that if I acted alive
He'd never stop and kill me.
Funny thing, I can't remember
Anything harder than trying to play dead
So as to avoid being murdered by my father.

Stop!

Stop! Stop what you're doing!
Stop! I mean you…you…you!
Take heed of what I say…
I miss you here today!
Don't you know how much I'm missing
Here today? Today…Today…Today!
You're the one I dream about every night
When I turn out the light.
No, nothing feels alright without YOU.
I wish I knew just what to do,
I'm saving all of my Love for you.
So come and take my hand
We'll leave behind all that we can
And take a leap of faith…faith…faith
That will turn out right real soon.
So let me say to you
I'm saving all my Love for you.
You're always in my heart
I knew it from the start
I'm saving all my Love for you.
So come and take my hand
We'll leave behind all that we can
And take a leap of faith
That all will turn out right real soon.
You're always in my heart
I knew it from the start
I'm saving all my Love for you…You…YOU!

Summer Tyme at Last

It's taken so long for summer to get here
It's warm and it's sunny, the skies are nice and clear,
I want to go outside and get myself some sun
Summer's the best season for each and everyone,
The lawn is growing in my favorite shade of green
It's finally growing now where once the snow had been,
I can see the animals on the ground and in the air
They're searching for the food that they've buried there,
Outside the kids are playing and finally having fun
They are oh, so happy summer vacation has begun,
The weather is so nice that we go walking to the park
The days are so much longer now until it gets so dark,
Everywhere I look people are in their summer clothes
Children are busy flying kites in the wind as she does blow,
Over at the pond people are catching fish
Some are skipping stones as they make a secret wish,
You can look around and see the people with their pets
They are all so happy, this good as summer gets,
Any where you look there are people everywhere
So stop and take a breath of the warm fresh summer air.

It is another cold Summer day again. It seems
More like a day in the middle of Spring than a
Day in the middle of the Summer. It is another
Tyme when you need long pants and a sweatshirt
Or even a light jacket. It is a surprise in the midst
Of our week, for sure. It is a nice way to break
Up the days when the heat is so strong and very
Muggy. On days like today, it can seem like an
Old friend. Easy to deal with and a nice break
When the heat is so strong and very unbearable.
My favorite way to end a long, hot day is to go
And crawl into a nice, cold bed where you need
Blankets to keep you warm through the night.
As sure as tomorrow will come, the hot, sweaty
Days of Summer will return too.

Swan Lake

One day when I was back in High School,
I went swimming and boating with a couple
Of friends. We had had a great day up until
They talked me into some water skiing. I can
Remember how it had taken me several Tymes
To get up on my feet. The sun was shining
And the water was warm and as usual I was
Wearing a pair of cut offs, you know the ones
That you fray to look cool like everybody else.
They were unusually tight and I remember
Having gotten up on the skis and was happy
As a lark skiing around Swan Lake. I can
Remember smiling to my friends in the boat
As I cruised around the turns. But for some
Reason I hit a wave wrong and suddenly I
Spun out of control. The boat was going so
Fast that as I hit the water one half of my
Shorts went one way and the other half of
My shorts went the other way. I tried to
Reach for them, but both halves went under
Which left me climbing into the boat butt
Naked and very embarrassed as could be.
I got to spend the rest of the day wrapped
In a beach towel. How embarrassing!
When I got back to shore someone yelled
Out, "That's what you get for wearing your
Clothes so tight!"

Thank Heavens

Now I lay me down to sleep
As the dark moves in and darkness creeps
I say my prayers to our God above
I'm so thankful for the ones I Love
He holds us gently in his hands
As evening closes in across the land
He protects us all and keeps us safe
From the devil, demons and other wraiths
We pay him homage when we go to church
To keep us strong when in our souls we search
He made us the wind, the Earth and sky
In a place where the sun and moon can fly
He made us a place where we can live
In a space where we will all survive
He gave us the plants, animals and the Earth
Where we can grow and thrive in mirth.

Thankful

When this world has me feeling low
There's only one place that I need to go,
Away from the things that make me blue,
I just need to spend some more Tyme with you.
You make me strong when you hold my hand,
You have a way of making me feel so grand.
I just stare into your eyes of brown,
And suddenly I'm no longer feeling so down.
And if by chance I see you smile,
My depression will leave me for a while.
You're the one that I truly care for and Love,
God sent you to me from heaven above.
And when the day finally comes to an end,
I'll curl up next to you my friend.
Then I'll give you just a little kiss,
And it will fill my heart with bliss.
With just enough Love to end my day,
I'm so thankful to you in every way.

At the end of the evening
I hope that I am lying next to you
Just holding you so nice and tight
And taking in the very beat of your heart.
I know that we have finally become one:
One heart, one soul, one Love…
Our hearts beat together as one.
We are two people just trying to get through.
We are so much more than friends.
When my soul cries out, it cries to YOU.
Hear me my darling, HEAR ME,
I Love you so very much more
Than I thought possible
To care for anyone again.
So just take my hand
And we'll ride through
The darkened evening sky
Till we find the edge of night.

The Lead Touch

Most everyone is familiar with the story of
King Midas having the golden touch, but
Few people really know about my secret
Affliction of having the lead touch…Now
Let me be frank with you…this doesn't
Mean that everything I touch necessarily
Turns to lead, I just mean that I have the
Ability to take an ordinary thing and I am
Damned if I don't break it when I pick it
Up or try to move it ever so carefully and
Whoops, there it goes…BROKEN! I'm
Not kidding either. I'm constantly told by
My husband, "Don't touch that. You know
Your luck…you'll break that!" And look
I just did. This is also true of my touching
Other people's things. If I touch something
Even by accident, I will still break it. How?
I don't know, I just do. Those around me
Are constantly reminding me of this too.
"Remember the last Tyme I told you not to
Touch something and you didn't listen to me
And you broke it? You keep those little lead
Touch hands of yours off of it." And I don't
And yeah, I know, wrong again and I broke
Something. There's an old sign that says,
"You break it…you bought it." That was in
Reference to me, King of the Lead Touch.
Stay away, stay very far away unless you
Have the money to pay for it. I never listen
And I'm constantly paying for it…literally.

The Light of My Life

You are the reason that I am here
And the reason I Love you so very much.
You are the light that guides me to my
Happiness and joy each and every day.
Even when the path we're on takes a turn
For a fork in the road, you are there to lead
Me the way back to my sanity. I know
That Tymes the light seems to dim and
That our path seems to have led us astray
But instead of getting lost and going in
Circles, your Love leads me down the
Path to the light we need to guide us back
To reality. Your smiling face is the one
That I choose to spend not only the good
And bad days with, but all of the others too.
Your comforting words and affection are
The force that keeps me alive. SomeTymes
Trying to find light that keeps us whole
Can become difficult when our lives become
A mess. It is someTymes easier to let faith
Take the reigns and turn to God for strength,
Forgiveness and guidance. SomeTymes all
We really need is to find our way back to a
Steady life is to let our friends and God
Keep us in the glory of their light and keep
Us from the darkness and sadness that we
Are going through. SomeTymes we just
Need to remember to have faith.

The New Girl in Town

Kaydee is my wonderful cat...She has
Gotten to be very social since our other
Cat Aimee has passed. She used to be
Very quiet and never spent too much
Tyme with me. That's because she used
To spend all of her Tyme teasing and
Chasing Aimee all around the house.
Since Aimee is gone she has no one to
Chase around anymore. She has also
Become more of a lap cat too. Before
Aimee passed away she was very quiet
And reserved animal who never really
Did much except terrorize the other cat.
Now, she has become very vocal and
Clings to me all of the Tyme. She is
Very much a different cat now that she
Is all alone. She has become very needy
And wants to have all of my attention
All of the Tyme. It's funny but she never
Made any noise before. Now though she
Has made up for lost Tyme in the talking
Department. She never wanted to sit
With me. Now she wants to to be petted
All of the Tyme and demands to sit on my
Lap and soak up all of my attention 24/7.
What a silly little girl.

The Sandbox

When I was just a little tyke, I used to Love
Playing in a sandbox. Once a year the city
Would fill your sandbox for the price of a
Couple of dollars. My best friends and I
Would play for hours in our old tire that we
Had converted into a sandbox. One of our
Favorite games to play in the sandbox was
Dairy Queen. We would pretend that we
Were making banana splits, ice cream cones
Floats, and sundaes. Oh, what fun we had
Getting to make ice cream cones for our
Friends. We liked to build things made of
Sand and water too. We would build roads
And homes for our action figures and our
Toy cars. My favorite thing was to play in
The sand box with my friends Patty, Peggy
Brenda and Kim. We always had a great
Tyme. We spent hours just pretending we
Were working at Dairy Queen making some
Treats for everyone. Hot fudge sundaes were
always a favorite of mine. SomeTymes we
Played at Patty and Peggy's sandbox and
Sometimes we played in ours, but we always
Had a lot of fun. Mmmmm, just thinking
About all that ice cream makes me want an
Ice cream cone right now.

The Wind

There's nothing quite like the wind in the trees
It moves the air with a gentle breeze.
The wind helps plants to move their pollen
As it carries the seeds when they have fallen.
The air smells fresh and the wind is clean
It blows the grass and things so green.
It tickles as it moves across your face
SomeTymes it blows at a tremendous pace.
It moves the air that we call the clouds
Into a storm when the wind gets loud.
It sends the raindrops to the ground
It blows the leaves with a rustling sound.
It moves the air when the thunder howls
It's place to fly for birds and fowl.
It moves it's oxygen as it flows through the sky
For without the wind things couldn't fly.
It provides a space for planes to go
As it's pressure moves from high to low.
It causes waves to move over the ocean
In a sound so free as they cause it's motion.

Ton of Bricks

Sometymes my pain is so overwhelming
That all I can do is just turn on the loudest
And heaviest music that I can find. Then
I sit back and let the onslaught of my brain
Begin. I ache as the beats that are playing
Hit me like a ton of bricks. I ache from the
Top of my head to the bottom of my feet.
I feel nothing but loud, huge heavy waves
Of bass. For a while my soul is appeased
Of the pain it is feeling. After what seems
To be eons, I take all of the energy from
The music and absorb it into my psyche
So I have an overzealous amount of power
Left in my memories to start a funeral pyre
The size of evermore. When it finally
Explodes all creatures of the Earth will
Take note as a day the Earth shook from
One polar end of the globe to the other.

True Friendship

Friendship is an important necessity to
Keeping us sane and grounded. As the
World spins into chaos and craziness,
Our friends can be a source of stability.
SomeTymes the world gets to be such
A gigantic mess that we get lost in all
Of the bad things that are occurring in
Our lives. We tend to forget about all
Of the good things that are happening
Each and every day. Darkness seems
To be overshadowing the ones that are
Positive and optimistic. Reality speaks
Of remembering all the negative. These
Are the moments that we recall as they
Are the ones that speak the loudest.
Often these are the Tymes when we feel
All alone and the moments we sense
That we can't go on. It is at these Tymes
We can find happiness and joy when we
Turn away from all of the negative things
That hold us down and we seek the help
Of others. Friends are with us when we
Are flying high in happiness, but there
Are Tymes we need to remember that
Real friends aren't there just when we
Are feeling low. They are there to help
Us enjoy each and every moment that
We experience...good, bad or indifferent.
Here's to friends that help us through and
Give us strength and Love each and every
Day.

Tyme to Go

Outside the trees are bare and lonely
The sky is covered up with clouds,
I'm so sick of this long winter
I want to scream it out so loud.
Out of doors the airs so cold and frosty
It can chill you to the bone,
I hear we'll get more snow tonight
It makes me want to groan.
I look up to the gray skies
These cold days go on and on,
Seems like forever since I've seen the sun
But one day soon they'll be gone.
I like to see some flowers growing
I'm tired of walking through the snow,
I'd rather be outside today
This crappy weather's got to go.
I hope the weather will change soon
This Winter Tyme is not my thing,
I'm ready for our next season
I hope tomorrow brings the Spring.

Until the End

Your Love
Is like a light,
It shines like a beacon
All through the night,
Because when I'm lost
And I'm feeling cold,
You're the one I need
Love never grows old.
Your face
Your beautiful smile,
Takes my breath away
For just a little while.
Because when you're near
You hold onto my hand,
It lifts up my mood
It makes me feel so grand.
So take my Love
And hold it so strong,
I'll guide you through life
And I won't steer you wrong.
I miss you my Love
I miss you're light,
For it guides me through life
And makes everything right.
Oh, we were so close
So don't let it end,
I'll be there for you
From now till the end.

Wait and See

I looked outside to start my day,
But everything was dull and gray.
No, there wasn't any sun to see,
Oh, what a treacherous day indeed.
It feels like I've lost my soul,
It's like my heart was made of coal.
Nothing to see, nothing shines,
Just like a dark moment in a darker Tyme.
So I sit back down to meditate,
And I call out to the god of Fate.
I begged him for a day of sun,
A day that's Loved by everyone.
A day that's warm and not too hot,
I asked for a day to hit the spot.
But he said there's nothing he could do,
So I just go on feeling blue.
Perhaps tomorrow my day will better be,
I guess I'll just have to wait and see.

Weeds

Life is like a garden,
It grows when you give
It the attention that it needs.
But depression is like a weed
In your garden. It grows in your
Garden even though you are trying
To get rid of it. You can take Tyme to
Pull on it and cut it down, but if you aren't
Careful it comes right back. It can drown out
The healthy parts of your garden and drown it over
And over again and again and again. The easiest of
Ways to destroy it is to tend to it daily. Like a good part
Of your garden you need to give it constant attention too.
The best thing you can do to keep it under control is to
Give it the same amount of tending to as you do the
Parts of your garden that you Love. Every Tyme
You see it, pull it, yank it and throw it away
So it doesn't take over your garden's
Life and cause it to take over the
Parts of your garden that you
Love and appreciate and
Keep your eyes on
It and remember
If you don't
You'll be
Sorry!

You make me feel so special and Loved
With all of the thoughtful things that you
Do for me. I am never ceased to be
Amazed at just how lucky I am to have
You in my life. Thoughtful words and
Gestures tell me just how much you care
For me each and every day. You make
Me feel so completely Loved and cared
For. I feel like I am the luckiest person
In the world to have you in my life. You
Do so many nice things for me and I Love
You for it. If only the planet was filled
With such thoughtful and Loving people, what
A wonderful world it would be!

As I lay my head down on my pillow
I turn off the lights and wait for my
Eyes to adjust to the darkness all
Around me. I can vaguely see the
Outline of the window so I can open
It to let the light of the moon shine
Through. I can begin to see the stars
That are all around me. Some of the
Stars are brighter than the others. I
Look up at the moon and see that he
Is smiling at everything in the sky.
Even the clouds that pass over it
Seem to be welcoming his light from
Above. I stare up at the spaces that
Are in between the stars and wonder
Why there is so much space out there.
There is so much space that goes on
And on eternally and without end. I
Wonder why God made so much space
In between and why even when it is
Dark you can still see the outlines of
The rest of the world as she rests and
Waits for the next day to come forth
With the rising of the sun.

With You

I'd like to simply go back in Tyme
I'd relive the days that you were mine.
I'd spend every moment like it was my last
I'd forget the mistakes we'd made in the past.
I'd kiss you forever and hold you just right
I'd never let you go far from my sight.
I'd remember the fun Tymes we had made
I'd go walking with you or sit in the shade.
I'd take your hand and hold it in mine
I'd hold you in my arms with all my free Tyme.
I'd relive the moments that we made Love
I'd thank God for sending you from above.
I'd remember the moments when we first kissed
I'd relive the first night we found our bliss.
I'd redo every moment that we had been through
I'd simply spend all of my lifeTyme with you.

Without a Word

SomeTymes the simplest acts of kindness
Can say more that the most extravagant of
Gifts could ever say…
SomeTymes I just don't know just what to
Say without saying the words that I Love you.
SomeTymes I just don't know what I can do
Just to show you how much you mean to me.
It is so very much more than I thought I had
Left in myself to Love another person,
So very much indeed…
I wish I knew a way to give more than I do,
I want to give my all to you…
And if there comes a day when I think that I
Have run out of things to say,
I will remind myself that someTymes the most
Is said without saying anything at all…
Without a word

Without You

I remember the Tymes when we were friends
It seemed like the nights would never end.
You made me feel like my soul was free
Just spending Tyme with you was all I'd need.
We'd sit around and drink and we'd sigh
Just hanging with you made me feel so high.
Now I'm feeling so lost and feeling so blue
Because you left me alone to live without you.
Without you my life's full of tension
I'm feeling way too low to mention.
You won't answer my calls by phone
Without your friendship I feel so alone.
We had such fun just the three of us
But then you threw me under the bus.
You left me feeling so alone and sad
If you came back I'd be feeling so glad.
You left me here in silent repose
Still the gate to my heart will never close.
Maybe one day you'll come back once more
So until then I'll keep an open door.

You

You are the reason that I live,
You have so much to give.
You fill my life with Love,
You are as gentle as a dove.
You have a great big heart,
You Loved me from the start.
You fill my soul with glee,
You are as handsome as can be.
You are so giving and so kind,
You make me happy that you're mine.
You are so gentle and so caring,
You are so precious and so sharing.
You are the one I Love to kiss,
You fill my heart with bliss.
You are the one I will grow old with,
You are the one I share my soul with.
You are always there to share a smile,
You make my life worth while.
You make my future bright,
You are my guiding light.
You will be with me till the end,
You are my greatest friend.

Printed in the United States
By Bookmasters